Also by Sheleana Aiyana

Becoming the One

ISBN 978-1-7972-2242-4

Manufactured in China.

MIX
Paper | Supporting responsible forestry
FSC™ C008047
www.fsc.org

Design by Pamela Geismar.

Typesetting in Garamond 3 and Brandon Grotesque.

This book contains advice and information relating to health and interpersonal well-being. It is not intended to replace medical or psychotherapeutic advice and should be used to supplement rather than replace any needed care by your doctor or mental health professional. While all efforts have been made to ensure accuracy of the information contained in this book as of date of publication, the publisher and the author are not responsible for any adverse effects or consequences that may occur as a result of applying the methods suggested in this book.

10 9 8 7 6 5 4 3 2 1

Chronicle books and gifts are available at special quantity discounts to corporations, professional associations, literacy programs, and other organizations. For details and discount information, please contact our premiums department at corporatesales@chroniclebooks.com or at 1-800-759-0190.

CHRONICLE PRISM

Chronicle Prism is an imprint of
Chronicle Books LLC
680 Second Street
San Francisco, California 94107

www.chronicleprism.com

MW00380635

Mend Your Relationship Patterns and Reclaim Your Self

BECOMING THE ONE

A GUIDED JOURNAL

SHELEANA AIYANA

Founder of Rising Woman

CHRONICLE PRISM

Dedicated to the brave and beautiful souls
willing to dive deep within.

You are making this world a better place.

Introduction   7

INTRODUCTION

MANY OF US HAVE BEEN CONDITIONED TO BELIEVE THAT to be loved, we must bend, shape-shift, and, ultimately, change who we are. When we strive to win or earn love, we may find ourselves self-abandoning, chasing unavailable partners on a never-ending roller coaster of hot and cold relationships, or struggling to get past the initial dating phase. But true love is birthed from a place of self-acceptance, when we are able to bring our whole and most authentic expression to our relationships. *Knowing ourselves is what makes this possible.*

In love, we get to choose how we show up, how we respond to each new twist and turn, what we say yes to, and when to go deeper or in a different direction. But the rest isn't up to us. When a partner will come into our lives, when a relationship will end, loss, death, massive life change—this is the unpredictability of life. That is why the relationship we have with *ourselves* is foundational and vital to living a life that reflects our essence and what we truly desire.

This is an invitation to reclaim the parts of yourself that you may have lost touch with and create a deeper relationship to your own heart. To discover what is important to you, challenge your beliefs around love, and consciously choose the life you want. This is what it means to become *the one*.

The journey you are about to embark on within these pages is one of healing—healing old wounds, projections, patterns, and the stories we've allowed to shape our self-worth. The point of healing is not to get something or find someone, but to relax into the life that is here in front of us, so we can cultivate true richness within ourselves, our friendships, and our communities. It is about building a safe and secure home within our own hearts and trusting that we are loved and worthy of all the beauty life has to offer, whether we are in a relationship or not.

My own personal history is laced with childhood abandonment, growing up in foster homes, and eventually finding myself in addiction and toxic relationship cycles that left me with a brutally defended heart. The inner work this journal will guide you through is the same work that saved my life. If you've come from a painful history of trauma or family dysfunction, or are carrying stories of unworthiness, navigating and letting love in can be incredibly challenging. My prayer is that this journal will help you feel closer to yourself and more ready to embody a full *yes* to life and love in all its forms.

Healing patterns and forging a deeper relationship to self are not linear. There's no formula or sure path. Rather, we are thrust into the unknown of our inner wildness and asked to gather the truth of who we are. While there's no magic pill, there are certainly tools and rituals that can lighten the load, support you in your quest, and reduce the amount of resistance you'll encounter along the way. Healing is not about changing the core of who we are but rather about accepting the beauty in our humanity. It is recognizing that our unique story, our gifts, our mistakes, life lessons, and relationship histories are all a part of the brilliance we are here to experience. No matter our age, there is always a deeper layer we can reach.

I am the founder of Rising Woman, and over the years I have been blessed with a readership of over three million people around the world. My studies and training in conscious relationship, somatic healing, inherited family trauma, and inner-child work and my immersion in plant medicine and inner journeying have led me to create the book and online program *Becoming the One*—the inspiration for this journal. Over thirty thousand people from 146 countries have gone through this program, which continues to resonate with hearts and souls worldwide.

My intention with this journal is to help you gently and compassionately explore your patterns, learn new ways to connect with yourself on an emotional and spiritual level, and develop a crystal-clear vision of the life you want to create. If you are reading *Becoming the One*, you may choose to use this journal in tandem with the book or on its own. Throughout, you will find reflective writing prompts, somatic exercises, and peaceful practices you can do in nature to reconnect with the elements. There are also rituals for self-care, altar building, herbal teas and flower baths, and self-soothing meditations to help you align with the creative energy that lives within you and awaken your intuition.

This journal is meant to usher you into greater self-awareness. At times, you may find yourself feeling heavy or needing time to process. Take as much time as you need and go at your own pace. If at any point you feel overwhelmed, consider calling on a healer, guide, or counselor you trust for support.

Whether you are single, in a relationship, or somewhere in between, these practices will help you embody the qualities you may have been seeking outside of yourself or in a partner and *become the one* for yourself, fully expressed in your own truth, core values, and inner wisdom.

BECOMING THE ONE IS . . .

Building a safe and secure relationship to self

Transforming your relationship patterns

Learning how to show up authentically in a relationship

Clearing old wounds and making peace with your past

Doing the foundational work to prepare you
for a conscious relationship

Reaching a place of self-acceptance and compassion
for all of your past selves

Remembering your oneness with all living beings
in this great universe

A NOTE BEFORE YOU BEGIN

CREATE A JOURNALING RITUAL

Make writing within this journal a part of your daily or weekly habit. Set aside a special time of day and ritualize it by preparing yourself a nice cup of tea or fruit-infused water and lighting a candle.

FIND A RITUAL SPOT IN NATURE

Choose a place in nature that will be your "ritual spot" throughout your journey. To find your spot, take a walk somewhere in nature that is close enough for you to visit frequently. Let your intuition and body guide you. If there's a place that evokes a sense of safety and inner peace, that just may be your ritual spot! It may be a park bench, under a special tree, in a meadow, near a running creek, or wherever calls to you. If nature is not easily accessible to you, find a space within your home that makes you feel calm and safe, bring plants into your environment, or listen to nature sounds. You can go to this place often to practice many of the nature meditations, exercises, and guided visualizations within these pages. You may choose to play non-lyrical music or go to sheleanaaiyana.com/journal to listen to the audio recordings of each meditation.

BE GENTLE WITH YOURSELF

Remember that healing is not a race. As you uncover deeper layers of your being, bring tenderness and compassion to each step. This work requires radical honesty, so if you find yourself going into self-blame about your past, know that you were doing your best with what you had at the time. The inner work isn't meant to make you feel guilty or wrong, but to empower you. Self-awareness must be paired with warmth and kindness.

COME BACK TO YOUR JOURNAL ENTRIES

I recommend you return to your entries often and review what you wrote. You may find that as you go deeper into your own practice of self-awareness, new insights come, and you may want to do the prompts over again.

GROUNDING MEDITATION

Before you start a new chapter or if you feel resistance to delving into a particular topic, take a quiet moment in nature, under a tree, or in your ritual spot at home to practice this grounding meditation. If you have little ones around, you can invite them to imagine that they are a tree with you and speak this visualization out loud.

> *Sit with your eyes closed, and imagine that you are part of a tree, with roots growing from the bottom of your feet down into the earth.*
>
> *The earth's cool and rich reddish-brown soil feels calming beneath you.*
>
> *Place your hands on your heart and take a few slow breaths in and out.*
>
> *On each inhale, breathe in safety.*
>
> *On each exhale, breathe out love.*
>
> *As you breathe, feel the roots of the tree holding you in this present moment.*
>
> *Feel the sense of safety, shade, and nourishment the tree is offering you and give thanks.*
>
> *Offer yourself gratitude for taking this time to center yourself.*
>
> *Open your eyes and take in your surroundings. Say to yourself, "I am safe, I am grounded, I am present."*

When you are ready, stretch your limbs and wiggle your toes as you take note of a few colors in your environment.

Take a few slow breaths and start your journaling.

Healing is not about changing the core
of who we are, but rather about accepting
the beauty in our humanity.

1

YOUR
HEALING PATH

WHEN YOU HEAR THE WORD *HEALING*, WHAT COMES TO mind first? Perhaps this word has a positive connotation for you, or maybe, like many others, you imagine something broken or in need of fixing. While it's true that many of us who seek out healing are indeed looking for change of some sort, the energy we bring to this work matters. In this section, we're going to explore our relationship to healing and the meaning we make of our own story. What you believe about yourself shapes your inner reality and self-esteem. That energy is then transmitted out into the world and impacts all aspects of your life. Rather than approaching this work from the stance that you need to change who you are, we're going to reframe this process as one of self-acceptance, self-love, and integration.

We are all shaped by our histories. Our family system, our past relationships, the authority figures we have growing up, and the media we take in all influence our beliefs about life, safety, relationships, and love. As we examine our conditioning, we can learn to release certain thought patterns, beliefs, or stories that no longer belong to us anymore.

YOUR RELATIONSHIP TO HEALING

Complete the following sentences by writing the first thoughts that come to mind. All the sentence stems found throughout this journal are designed to help you get out of your own way and uncover beliefs beneath the surface of your logical mind. Whenever you are given one of these prompts, don't think about your answers too much, just allow yourself to flow through the sentences, and later you can return to explore what hidden messages surface. Write until you are empty and have poured everything onto the page.

If you don't particularly resonate with a sentence stem, I still encourage you to engage the question with curiosity. You may be surprised by what you uncover when you allow yourself to be radically honest and free from judgment. There are no right or wrong answers, and there's nothing to feel ashamed of. The more honest you are with yourself, the more clarity you will gain, so be open!

My intention for beginning the *Becoming the One* journal is:

I want to do the inner work because:

The tone of my inner self-talk is usually:

The meaning I assign to my relationship status is:

A quality I wish to embody more of in my life is:

Something I want to experience more of in my relationships is:

Something I'd really like to see change in my relationships is:

I will know when I'm healing because:

I hope the inner work will help transform my life in these ways:

On a scale of 1 to 10, how willing am I to be radically honest with myself and to take responsibility for my patterns?

1   2   3   4   5   6   7   8   9   10

A part of starting this journey that scares me is:

....

....

....

....

....

....

....

I will practice self-care and gentleness with myself as I move through this journal by:

....

....

....

....

....

....

....

....

FREE-JOURNAL

Write about where you're at today in your relationships, health, career, finances, friendships, community, personal growth, and all areas of your life. Don't hold back here; write down anything that wants to come up. Finish this with a vision for your future self. What are your deepest desires and dreams? How do you want to feel, what energy will you embody, and how will you express yourself?

Our relationship to self ripples out and
touches every aspect of our lives. Spirit, nature,
self, and other are all interconnected.

2

EXPLORING
YOUR RELATIONSHIP
TO SELF

WHEN WE HEAR THE TERM *CONSCIOUS RELATIONSHIP*, our first association is likely a couple. But the reality is, building a conscious relationship starts with *you*. A healthy and grounded relationship to self is the foundation from which all other relationships can bloom.

you

spirit

other

nature

We can build beautiful partnerships with others only when we know ourselves, what we stand for, and what we want. In the pages to come, you will begin to explore your origin story—the past experiences that have shaped what you believe to be true about love, relationships, and yourself.

You will also learn to recognize whether your desires and actions are coming from a place of fear or a place of love by becoming a *witness to your thoughts*. Rather than believing every thought, you can start to create distance between you and your thoughts. As you train yourself to observe your mind, you will then be able to determine what is true and what is simply passing through.

OBSERVE YOUR MIND

Take a moment to pause. What thoughts are coming up?

_____

_____

_____

_____

_____

_____

_____

_____

Tune in to your body. Are these thoughts coming from love or fear?

_____

_____

_____

_____

_____

_____

_____

_____

_____

Where does this thought originate from? Where did you learn this?

Is this thought self-loving, or self-harming?

Is this thought true? Why or why not?

....

....

....

....

....

....

....

....

....

....

How can you shift this thought to reflect more self-compassion and self-acceptance?

....

....

....

....

....

....

....

....

....

....

....

OBSERVING YOUR ATTRACTIONS

It's true that you cannot choose who you are attracted to, and yet, your attractions can and will transform as you embody more of your wholeness.

When we are in a state of insecurity or feeling unworthy, we're much more likely to be drawn to chaotic or unstable relationship dynamics. As we begin to increase our confidence and self-knowledge, we will find that any lingering turn-on from chasing unavailable or unattainable partners dissipates, and we begin to feel a sense of neutrality toward this archetype. In essence, healing our attractions is about healing our own wounds that cause us to overextend and contort ourselves to gain approval and love. Rather than fighting to be chosen, we can claim the power to choose a partnership that mirrors the rich relationship we've built within our own hearts.

The next few journaling prompts are designed to help you observe what drives your current attractions and romantic connections to others. There is no judgment in this; you are simply getting to know yourself better.

The qualities in others I tend to be most attracted to are:

....

....

....

....

....

....

....

The qualities I tend to find myself least attracted to are:

....

....

....

....

....

....

....

....

....

The qualities I often feel are missing in my partnerships are:

....

....

....

....

....

....

....

....

....

....

....

SELF-DATING
TO BUILD A SECURE SELF

Learning to cherish your own company is vital to becoming the one. If you already enjoy your alone time, then you're invited to expand and get creative with the ways you spend that time. If you currently struggle to be alone or often feel a sense of loneliness, establishing a self-dating practice may be incredibly liberating for you.

The idea here isn't to strive to love being alone all the time—we are human after all; we are wired for connection! Craving and seeking community, friendship, and romantic love is a natural part of our journey on this earth. The purpose of this practice isn't to rid you of these longings, but to deepen your capacity to feel at home with yourself no matter where you are in life.

Set aside some time each week, or a few times per month as your schedule permits, to create your self-dating practice. If you have children and are unable to access childcare or community support, it's okay to schedule shorter blocks. If you have the space, you can be more elaborate.

Beyond just carving out space for yourself, you must also consider the quality of time spent on your own. Does technology play a big role? Are you often filling the space with distractions? The more intentional you become with this practice, the more doors to self-discovery, confidence, and inner strength you will uncover.

SELF-DATE IDEAS

- **Make yourself** a beautiful loose-leaf tea, light a candle, and read a book or listen to music.

- **Go see** a movie you've been wanting to watch. Buy yourself popcorn or bring a healthy snack.

- **Prepare** a delicious meal that you wouldn't normally prepare, just for yourself. Take time to enjoy the process and set the table beautifully as if you are having a guest over—and then enjoy!

- **Take yourself** on a nature walk, without looking at your phone or listening to music. Bring a childlike wonder and curiosity to your experience. Slow down and notice the little things, breathe in the fresh air, relish the sights around you.

- **Dine solo** at your favorite restaurant or somewhere you've always wanted to try.

- **Attend** a group class for yoga, dance, art, a hobby you're curious to try, or something you've loved but haven't created space for in a while.

Complete the following sentence stems. *Remember, with sentence stems, you are tapping into your unconscious belief systems. Don't overthink your answers or try to formulate a response. Even if a question doesn't speak to you, simply free-flow with whatever comes and write it down until you feel empty.*

I'm afraid to be alone because:

....

....

....

....

....

....

....

I'm afraid of commitment because:

....

....

....

....

....

....

....

....

I'm afraid to be in a relationship because:

....

....

....

....

....

....

....

I feel most like "myself" when:

....

....

....

....

....

....

I feel least like "myself" when:

....

....

....

....

....

....

....

I spend most of my alone time doing:

My relationship to nature looks and feels like:

I connect to nature in these ways:

....

....

....

....

....

....

My relationship to technology looks and feels like:

....

....

....

....

....

....

Something I'd like to shift about my relationship to technology is:

....

....

....

....

....

....

YOUR RELATIONSHIP TO
FOOD AND YOUR BODY

For many of us, food and our bodies may have negative associations that seem normal because of societal beauty standards. In this section, explore how you relate to nourishing yourself and how this impacts your self-esteem.

How would you describe your relationship to food and your body? (Is it energetically charged in a positive, neutral, or negative way?)

When you feel hunger, is your first instinct to nourish yourself, or do you feel concerned about weight and body image?

....
....
....
....
....
....
....
....
....
....

The way I view and treat my body affects my life in these ways:

....
....
....
....
....
....
....
....
....
....
....

YOUR SELF-IMAGE

If you were to describe yourself, what would you say? How would you describe your personality, talents, and weaknesses? Write about yourself in depth without a filter:

What do you love and celebrate about yourself?

When we are healing, we may fall into the
trap of thinking there are parts of our being
that need to be tucked away, but usually
the elements that we struggle with most are
also our medicine in this life.

3

SOMATIC HEALING AND EMOTIONAL ALCHEMY

MANY OF US EXPERIENCE A DISCONNECTION FROM OUR selves and our bodies at an early age, often relying on external authorities to tell us what to do and how to heal. We've been led to believe that only doctors or scientists can tell us what our bodies need. Systems that see us in parts and not as holistic beings intertwined with nature strip us of our power. As we regain sovereignty and take full responsibility for our bodies, we become rooted in our truth and our innate ability to heal ourselves.

Tuning in to your body gives you a direct line of communication to Spirit and your intuition. The more connected you are, the clearer your internal guidance will be within your relationships and in every area of your life. Plants, herbs, foods, and remedies may suddenly pop up in your thoughts or dreams or in a flash of insight. That is your body wisdom in action.

Your emotional well-being is reflected in the way you listen to and care for yourself. It is a constant, ever-changing practice of turning inward and finding your balance. The simple self-care rituals peppered throughout this journal will help you find your flow, so you may draw closer to the endless well of wisdom that you hold within you.

LISTENING TO YOUR BODY

Take a moment to sit in a quiet place and get into your body. Close your eyes and breathe deeply. Feel the way your chest rises with each breath. Feel your muscles and limbs expand and contract. Slowly move parts of your body, wiggling your toes and fingers, rolling your neck, and shrugging your shoulders. Gently begin asking your body a few questions:

When I'm stressed, I tend to hold energy in these parts of my body (such as shoulders, lower or upper back, hips, stomach, etc.):

....

....

....

....

....

....

....

....

When I am happy, or relaxed, I tend to feel it most in these parts of my body:

....

....

....

....

....

....

....

....

....

My body is asking for (for example, deep rest, nurturing warm foods, fresh fruits or leafy greens, calming movement, etc.):

....

....

....

....

....

....

....

....

....

I commit to incorporating these self-care rituals and practices for nurturing my body into my routine:

....

....

....

....

....

....

....

....

....

EMOTIONAL ALCHEMY

We are each made up of the four elements. Our personalities and emotional tendencies often reflect one element that we favor, while we are less tapped into other elements or are unaware they even exist within us. When we learn to no longer suppress sensations and emotions and instead welcome them, we can begin to express new or lost parts of ourselves that yearn to be shared with the world.

For a fire type, anger and boundaries may come more easily, while tenderness and vulnerability (associated with water) feel foreign. Someone more air-oriented may find dancing in the imaginal realms a breeze but struggle with earth traits like self-esteem or following a project through to completion. This is part of emotional alchemy.

ELEMENTS OF EMOTIONAL ALCHEMY

Fire: angry, confident, strong boundaries, joyful,
action-oriented, passionate, determined
When out of balance: hot-tempered, insensitive, self-loathing

Earth: high self-esteem, compassionate, intuitive,
practical, grounded, calm, stubborn, nurturing
When out of balance: worrisome, obsessive, self-critical

Air: creative, communicative, spiritual, adaptable,
playful, dreamy, friendly, intellectual
When out of balance: flighty, detached, ungrounded

Water: emotional, deep, transformative, wise,
visionary, sensitive, psychic, sensual
When out of balance: fearful, sad, overwhelmed with emotions

The element (fire, earth, air, water) I tend to relate to the most is:

The element I want to lean into and express more is (deeper intuition, higher self-esteem, speaking up and setting boundaries, vulnerability, etc.):

When I feel a big emotion or sensation in my body, rather than distract or numb, I'm going to (pause and breathe deeply, go for a nature walk, journal, play an uplifting song and dance through the energy, etc.):

_____

_____

_____

_____

_____

_____

_____

_____

_____

_____

_____

_____

_____

Complete the following sentence stems.

Anger is:

....

....

....

....

....

....

....

....

Sadness is:

....

....

....

....

....

....

....

....

....

FREE-JOURNAL

What did you discover from the sentence stems on anger and sadness? What beliefs are underneath those thoughts about emotional expression? What are you afraid might happen if you expressed more of your anger or sadness? What might happen if you gave yourself permission to express the emotions you avoid the most?

BEING WITH ANXIETY

Many of us struggle with anxiety without even realizing that's what we're experiencing. Tension, nervousness, overthinking, avoidance, and obsession are all expressions of anxiety. What is beneath the surface of anxiety?

We may avoid coming face-to-face with our anxiety out of fear that if we surrender to the feeling beneath it, we will be swallowed by an oceanic force of pain and never find our way back. But pain is a passage, not a prison. It's safe to surrender and allow yourself to go deeper within. Often when we are overcome with anxiety it's because we are resisting our reality on some level. Perhaps we need to release something we've been holding on to or accept a big change within our lives. The next time you experience waves of anxiety, find a comfortable place to sit or lie down and use the following meditation to return to your body and move through the emotion. Make room for whatever message wants to come forward.

A reminder that you may also listen to the audio version of this meditation and those found throughout this journal by going to sheleanaaiyana.com/journal.

How do you typically respond to anxious thoughts and feelings in the moment?

....

....

....

....

....

OCEANIC VISUALIZATION AND
SOMATIC MEDITATION FOR ANXIETY

Place a hand on your heart and belly . . .

Feel the rise and fall of your breath. Notice the sensations you feel in your chest, legs, arms, face, and throughout your body. Name them: tingly, tight, cool, warm, and so on.

Return to your breath . . .

Is it heavy or shallow? Simply notice. Next try to locate the anxious energy in your body. Does it have a shape, a color? If the anxiety had words for you, what would it say? Listen quietly; don't overthink or create a script.

Allow your anxiety to serve as a messenger . . .

When you receive the message, ask yourself, "What's the feeling underneath this anxiety?" Stay with your body. There's no need to run or shut down this feeling.

Visualize gentle ocean water washing over you . . .

Imagine your body being held and cleansed by the sea. With each wave that washes over you, imagine that you are giving whatever emotion came up for you to the waters.

With hands on your heart . . .

Thank your body for carrying you, your heart for beating, your breath for giving you life.

Slowly return to the space you are in . . .

Look around at your surroundings and say, "My body is a safe place. All of my emotions and sensations are welcome."

What did you discover during your meditation? What did you find beneath your anxiety?

....
....
....
....
....
....
....
....
....
....

LEARNING TO CHANNEL
YOUR ENERGY

Healing is an integrative process. It is about learning to channel our energy into the right places. It's a dance of the elements and an honoring of our unique gifts for the world. When we are healing, we may fall into the trap of thinking there are parts of our being that need to be tucked away, but usually the elements that we struggle with most are also our *medicine* in this life.

For those of us who have a lot of fire energy, we know this element can be expressed in destructive ways: lashing out, blaming, walling off, and pushing people away. The natural response is to try to put out the fire, but your fire is also your strength. It is the energy of passion, leadership, dedication, resilience, protection, boundaries, and transformation. We don't want to put it out; we want to learn how to tend to it while bringing in other elements to soften it. If we struggle with shame or guilt for having anger or expressing anger from a wounded place, our practice is to learn how to let our fire be a guiding light for others instead of burning everything down.

When we're working with a behavior or pattern that feels sticky, our tendency is to want to eliminate that part of ourselves altogether. Through welcoming these aspects of our nature, we heal.

Is there an element you struggle with or that is dominant within you?

....

....

....

....

....

....

....

....

....

How does it also act as medicine in your life and others' lives?
Remember, there is a gift and a shadow side to every expression!

....

....

....

....

....

....

....

....

....

ELEMENTAL ALTAR RITUAL

Building an altar to represent the elements you want to cultivate is a beautiful way to connect to Spirit and honor your process. If you don't already have an altar, find a place in your home that feels inviting and won't be disturbed by others. You could use a small table, a shelf, the top of your dresser, or even the base of your fireplace. Clean and beautify the space before you begin this ritual.

1. Place items on your altar that represent the emotional pattern you want to transform, such as earth (salt, sand, plants, rocks) or air (feathers, leaves, bells, incense).

2. Now add items that symbolize the elemental quality you want to call into your life (such as fire for stronger boundaries, earth for grounding, water for vulnerability, etc.).

3. Add a candle to your altar, and every time you light it, visualize embodying this element.

4. Bring in a flower or a bouquet to represent self-love and openness to new behaviors, thoughts, and transformation. Remember all parts of you are loveable, and the very thing you're battling may eventually be the energy you learn to channel as your gift.

5. With each full and new moon, remove or add items to represent the progress you've made or new aspects of yourself.

Keeping our inner child alive is essential to
living a life of full expression, joy, and play.
Embrace aging as a gift and keep your
spirit young.

4

CONNECTING
WITH YOUR
INNER CHILD

THINK OF YOUR *INNER CHILD* AS THE EVER-PRESENT, FULL-of-wonder, innocent, and wild little being you were before being conditioned by the world. Your inner child can also reflect the youngest part of you that may have strong demands, unmet needs, painful memories, and unresolved fears from the past, asking to be answered in your adult life.

When we are disconnected from our inner child, we may unknowingly be letting them drive the bus in our relationships—acting out, game-playing, responding immaturely during difficult situations—rather than our wise *inner adult*, who acts with self-awareness and confidence.

Doing inner-child work can help you access the voice of "little you" while integrating their being into your life more fully. This is how we begin to heal old wounds and step wholeheartedly into the present.

A RELATIONSHIP WITH YOUR INNER CHILD CAN HELP YOU . . .

Become more self-aware in relationships

Feel more secure and grounded

Tend to your vulnerable parts with wisdom

Express your emotions and needs more clearly

Feel whole, expressive, and open to the full spectrum of life

WAYS THE INNER CHILD ACTS OUT

Demanding versus making requests

Withholding, yelling, or blaming

Being self-focused rather than *we*-focused in conflict

Going after instant gratification

Procrastinating that leads to detrimental consequences

GETTING TO KNOW AND HEALING YOUR INNER CHILD

What are your earliest memories from childhood that stand out the most?

_____

_____

_____

_____

_____

_____

_____

What is something you used to love doing when you were a child? When is the last time you did that thing?

_____

_____

_____

_____

_____

_____

_____

What is something you were afraid of as a child? Did anyone provide you comfort or soothing during times of fear or distress?

What is something you were afraid of as a child? Did anyone provide
you comfort or soothing during times of fear or distress?

Did you receive warm and safe physical touch from your caregivers as
a child? What was that experience like for you?

What is something you wish you had received as a child, but didn't?

What is something you often yearn for in your relationships but don't feel you receive?

Do you see any correlation between these inner-child needs and your present longing?

What shows, movies, or other media did you consume when you were a child? What were the overall themes of this media? Did they feature relationships? What did those relationships look like?

When you close your eyes and imagine your inner child, how old are they? If your inner child had words for you today, what would they say? What are they feeling?

Embodying your inner adult, is there something you can offer your inner child today that they yearn for or are craving more of? (For example, nurturing, compassion, support, etc.)

What is something creative you loved doing when you were a child that you want to incorporate back into your life now?

SELF-SOOTHING INNER-CHILD PRACTICES

If you find yourself feeling anxious, overwhelmed, triggered, or shutting down, I welcome you to walk through the following practices. Any time you ignore, deny, or repress your emotions, your inner child suffers. As an adult, you can now begin to "parent" your own inner child by being self-loving and compassionate when emotions arise. These are tools you can draw on any time you need to self-soothe or slow down.

Pausing in the Storm

When we are in conflict or triggered, it can sometimes feel as if we are lost in a storm of emotions. Next time you feel swept up, take time to pause and ask yourself:

How old do I feel right now?
What does my inner child need in this moment?
How can my wise inner adult express my needs?

SELF-SOOTHING INNER-CHILD MEDITATION

Lie on your back with your eyes closed and place your hands on your belly and heart. Take a few deep breaths and breathe out any tension or tightness in your body. Begin to meditate.

Visualize light coming into your body as you feel yourself relaxing. Notice the sensations in your body and your emotions. Try to name them. Where do you feel them in your body?

Imagine little you at a young age, maybe between three and seven years old. Notice the environment that you and your inner child are in together. Are you in your old family home? Are you somewhere in nature?

Say hello to your inner child, ask them what they are feeling, and just listen. Maybe they have a lot to say, and maybe they are quiet. If they are quiet, simply be with them and hold them with love.

Invite your inner child to sit in your lap or snuggle with you. Allow them to choose. Let your inner child know that you are ready to reconnect with them. Assure them you're not going anywhere; you will always take care of them, listen, and give them space to express themselves.

Give your inner child a gift, such as a teddy bear, to symbolize the connection you now have. Visualize a warm embrace with them and breathe together. Imagine your inner child dissolving into you, as you become one.

Notice the sensations in your body. What are you feeling now? Notice the places in your body that feel safer and more relaxed. Take a few more deep breaths, wiggle your toes, and stretch your limbs. Open your eyes and look around the room. Notice your surroundings and say, "I am safe here."

Come back to this process any time you need to self-soothe.

DRAW YOUR INNER CHILD

In the space below, draw a picture that reflects your inner child. Using your nondominant hand will amplify this creative process and help bring your unconscious forward. That means if you are left-handed, you will draw with your right and vice versa. Tune inward and ask your inner child what they want to express. How are they feeling? What do they need? What message are they sending? This is not an analytical process but a creative one, so allow your hand to flow freely.

INNER-CHILD ALTAR RITUAL

If you have a photo of yourself from childhood, add it to your altar space alongside your elemental items. If you don't have a photo, you can use the drawing you made or choose an image that represents your inner child best.

Honor Your Inner Child: Choose a few devotional items that remind you of your innate essence and childlike spirit to place on the altar. You can add your favorite childhood objects, a teddy bear, a piece of clothing, a toy, or even candy.

Infuse Nature: Go for a walk in nature. If you find a leaf, a flower, or something natural that reminds you of your inner child, add this to your altar. When you feel ready to release it, return the item back to the outdoors.

Be Affirming: Take a few minutes to write little affirmations on pieces of paper or card stock and place them on the altar where they will be easily visible to you.

Write to Your Inner Child: Communicate words of love, affirmation, safety, and protection in a letter to yourself as a kid. Place it on your altar.

You will always belong to the earth. Find peace and safety within the wisdom of your own heart. Let the roots of the trees be your anchor and the stars in the sky remind you of your greatness. We are all connected in this precious life.

5

TENDING TO
THE ABANDONMENT
WOUND

RELATIONSHIPS HAVE THE POTENTIAL TO BRING US SO much joy, yet we may be struggling to experience our partnerships in full if we have unresolved needs from our earliest relationships—those with our parents or caregivers.

Many of us didn't receive the love and acceptance we yearned for when we were growing up. Generationally, and as a collective, we are continuously working to heal cycles passed down through family lines, whether a lack of care, nurturance, or attunement. If you were to interview your parents and grandparents about what it was like for them to grow up in their own families, you would more likely hear stories of neglect or physical abuse than those of open communication, warmth, and a loving environment.

As human beings, we all long to feel safe, connected, wanted, and loved. When this longing isn't fully met in childhood, it gets carried into our adult relationships, making shock waves in our romantic attempts to connect and sabotaging our desires for healthy and secure love. Underneath our defensiveness, need to be right, perfectionism, or impulse to chase unavailable love is often a tenderness and a vulnerability that begs, "Please don't leave me, I'm afraid to be abandoned." This is called the *abandonment wound*. While it may sound very literal, you don't have to have a story of being physically abandoned to carry this wound in your psyche and emotional body.

WAYS THE ABANDONMENT WOUND
CAN FORM

A traumatic birth where we were separated
from our mother for a time

A parent went away for a medical procedure or
extended period

A parent struggled with mental illness or addiction

A parent was not emotionally present

A parent was physically absent, passed away, or left

An unstable parent who went from warm to angry quickly

An overnight stay or being left at camp
before we were ready

Growing up with emotionally immature parents

WAYS THE ABANDONMENT WOUND
SHOWS UP IN RELATIONSHIP

Chasing unavailable love

Leaving before being left

Catastrophizing during conflict

Assuming the worst

Relationship anxiety

Struggling to trust safe and secure love

Neediness and making unrealistic demands

Jealousy and control

SELF-ABANDONMENT

When we're conditioned to feel as though love is scarce or unpredictable, our tendency can be to self-abandon to hold on to whatever love we can get. Healing the abandonment wound begins with acknowledging its presence in our life and understanding how it shows up. The real change happens when we learn to rewrite our beliefs around love, nurturance, trust, and self-care. Becoming the one is integrating new beliefs that love is indeed abundant rather than scarce and that we are inherently worthy of being seen, held, and cared for in all of our relationships.

Rather than self-abandoning in moments of heightened emotional intensity, the practices and journaling in this chapter will teach you to strengthen your sense of inner protection and nurturance so you can stay grounded in your true nature.

SELF-ABANDONMENT LOOKS LIKE . . .

Chasing unavailable partners

Neglecting our own self-care or health

Prioritizing others at the expense of our own well-being

Withholding our needs, truth, or experience

Hiding or holding back to keep love

Being "needless" in relationship

MEETING OUR WOUNDS WITH LOVE

Do you know your birth story?

_____

_____

_____

_____

_____

_____

_____

Write about what it was like for you in your home as a child. What was the emotional environment?

_____

_____

_____

_____

_____

_____

_____

_____

Did you feel safe with your caregivers growing up? Did you trust them with your secrets?

How were you received as a child when you expressed a big emotion like anger or sadness? Which emotions were considered bad? What emotions were acceptable in your household?

Were your caregivers consistently physically and emotionally present for you?

When in conflict as an adult, is your tendency to want to fix things right away or to retreat and withdraw?

Do you feel more comfortable in a giving or receiving role in relationships? Do you tend to attract partners who are highly independent or partners who seem to need you to take care of them (emotionally, financially, otherwise)?

After spending time with a romantic interest, what's it like for you to separate and take time apart? Do you feel anxious, lonely, content, relieved?

What was it like for you as a child when you had alone time? What is your experience of being alone as an adult? Do you see any connections between the two?

....

....

....

....

....

Complete the following sentence stems.

Love is:

....

....

....

....

....

Relationships are:

....

....

....

....

....

Men are:

....

....

....

....

....

Women are:

....

....

....

....

....

Trusting others is:

....

....

....

....

....

RETURNING TO PEACE NATURE MEDITATION

In times when you feel that your abandonment wound has been acti-
vated, go to your ritual spot in nature and either sit comfortably or put
a blanket down on the ground and lie flat on your back with your eyes
closed. Walk through this meditation to bring yourself back to center
and remember that love is abundant:

Place your hands on your heart. *Notice your breath and visualize
your entire being filled with pink mist.*

Visualize that pink mist *emanating around you, creating a sense of
healing, love, and self-protection.*

Notice any sounds. *Are there birds chirping, people laughing, leaves
rustling in the wind?*

As you slowly open your eyes, *take in the beauty around you and
give thanks to the earth for holding you. Feel the security of the ground
beneath you.*

Allow yourself to breathe *in the reality that you are taken care of
by all the elements, plants, and animal beings.*

Give thanks to the sky, *the stars, the sun and moon, the waters, the
trees, and all the plants and animals for their collaboration in sustain-
ing you in this life.*

Say this mantra *out loud or mentally: "I am deeply held and loved."*

COMMITTING TO YOURSELF

Are there areas in your life where you feel that you may be self-abandoning (work, relationship, family, etc.)? Write a self-love statement to yourself. Describe the different ways you are going to show up for yourself and prioritize your relationship to self. Create some short- and long-term goals:

Today I will:

This week I will:

This month I will:

_____

_____

_____

_____

_____

_____

This year I plan to:

_____

_____

_____

_____

_____

_____

_____

_____

_____

_____

_____

_____

_____

UPLIFTING SELF-ESTEEM CHAMOMILE ROSE BATH

Ritual is a beautiful way to honor our inner process and emotional state. It can bring us into reverence for our journey and help us find completion when the journey is coming to a close. If an ingredient doesn't call to you in this recipe or any of the recipes to follow, you can intuitively choose something that is safe to use and resonates with you most. More important than the ingredients is the act of ritual.

1 cup Epsom salts

1 small handful dried or fresh
    chamomile flowers

2 tablespoons almond oil

1 small handful organic dried roses

This particular bath recipe is meant to support you in self-nurturing and enhancing your self-esteem. Find some time in the evening to run a warm bath for yourself.

1. Add in the Epsom salts, chamomile flowers, and almond oil. The emotional healing properties of the chamomile flower bring calm, inner security, and relaxation. Next add the heart-opening rose petals, a flower often used in oils or essences to uplift self-esteem, confidence, and inner trust.

2. As you immerse yourself in the water, imagine all of your doubts and worries washing away. Invite the flowers in your bath to fill you with love and self-acceptance.

3. Once you feel calm and relaxed, hold a flower in the palm of your hands, close your eyes, and reflect on an intention you want to set or something you love about yourself. When you are ready, release this flower back into your warm bath. You may repeat this as many times as you like until you are completely surrounded by intentions and loving thoughts.

Note: With any bath ritual, it's important to buy organic flowers to avoid pesticides and toxins. If organic flowers aren't easily accessible to you, you can choose to use a bag or small handful of loose-leaf chamomile tea or loose-leaf tea with rose. Should it be difficult to source any of these flowers, simply use Epsom salts and almond oil.

With healing comes the wisdom and
capacity to embody maturity and embrace our
own inner mother and father.

6

EMBODYING YOUR DIVINE INNER PARENT

AS SMALL CHILDREN, WE SEE OUR PARENTS AS GODS, perfect in every way. We hold them in our minds on a pedestal. There is a saying from Gabor Maté that if a parent harms a child, the child will not blame the parent but themselves. This illustrates the unbreakable primal bond we all share with the ones who birth us into this world. As we grow older, we begin to realize our parents are not divine at all, and perhaps we are even deeply hurt, let down, neglected, or disappointed by them. This split can create a sense of confusion and even loss of trust in love itself. When left unhealed, the *mother and father wound*—the missing sense of protection, love, and acceptance we needed most as children—projects into our adult relationships, and we can find ourselves people pleasing, shutting down or avoiding conflict, struggling with low self-esteem, or drawn to codependent or chaotic dynamics.

Know that doing mother and father work is not about blaming or shaming our parents or confronting them about the past. This work is a vital part of individuating and maturing within ourselves so that we can release our parents from any conscious or unconscious contracts we've held them to that limit how deep we can go in our relationships with others.

This is work that we can all do, regardless of whether or not our parents were blatantly abusive or neglectful. It's possible to have a mother or father wound even in a family that was fairly peaceful. Often, we may struggle to acknowledge the ways our emotional needs weren't met and feel as though we are being ungrateful for all our parents gave us. What's true is that by burying any of these feelings, we inevitably give them more power to grow. The more we deny or suppress a thought or a feeling, the more it will come out sideways in our day-to-day lives and relationships. By giving ourselves permission to be radically honest, we then create a clear path to acceptance and forgiveness (which we will work on in the next chapter).

Our parents can certainly influence our development, but we ultimately determine who we become and what path we follow in life. We all see the world through our own lens and develop our own way of self-expression. As spiritual beings, we come to this planet with our own soul work to do, and our parents are simply stewards along the way.

If you are a parent yourself, do your best not to make this chapter about you as a parent, and instead focus on your own internal experience in your first family system. This alone will make you a more present and loving parent for your little ones. The fact that you are here doing this work in this very moment speaks volumes about how fortunate your children are to have you as a parent!

HEALING THE MOTHER-FATHER WOUND

We all mirror characteristics or qualities of our parents, and depending on how we relate to them, this may lead to living in self-rejection and shame with these parts of ourselves. By bringing our parents' traits into awareness, we begin to recognize how our relationships to our mother and father manifest in our present day. We can then see clearly the areas where we could embody more aspects of our nature and what we reject most in ourselves and others.

MOTHER

Something I dislike about my mother is:

....

....

....

....

....

....

Qualities of my mother that I reject in myself are:

....

....

....

....

....

....

Something I always wanted from my mother is:

....

....

....

....

....

Qualities that I like in my mother are:

....
....
....
....
....
....

I wish my mother was more:

....
....
....
....
....
....

I wish my mother was less:

....
....
....
....
....
....

FATHER

Something I dislike about my father is:

Qualities of my father that I reject in myself are:

Something I always wanted from my father is:

Qualities that I like in my father are:

_____
_____
_____
_____
_____
_____

I wish my father was more:

_____
_____
_____
_____
_____
_____

I wish my father was less:

_____
_____
_____
_____
_____
_____

SELF

The qualities from my mother and my father that I appreciate in myself are:

....

....

....

....

....

....

....

....

....

....

....

....

THE LETTER RITUAL

Write a letter to each of your parents. This letter is not to be sent to them under any circumstances. This is a personal ritual for you and your own healing work. Bring your most unfiltered, honest, and vulnerable self to this letter. Give yourself permission to be entitled to each and every feeling, desire, or disappointment that arises. You can either write this letter in the space provided in this journal or on a separate piece of paper. When finished, you may choose to place it on your altar and later burn the letter in the Accept and Release Moon Ritual (see page 117).

Heart-Opening Visualization

After you are done writing, go to your ritual spot in nature or find a quiet space in your home to sit with your eyes closed and practice a heart-opening visualization. Connect to the energy of the parent you wrote to and imagine them as a small child; feel their innocence. Visualize a green and pink mist, the colors associated with the heart chakra, emanating from your heart to theirs. Allow a sense of warmth and compassion to arise naturally and let it move through your entire body.

Closing Prayer

Place your hands on your heart and call in the energy of divine mother and father. Say out loud or in your head, "I release you from my expectations and the roles I've placed upon you. I am willing to see your innocence." As you sit in this quiet space, be present to the energy and visualize yourself rooted to the earth. Invite in the divine embrace of Spirit to hold and care for you. This loving connection is always available to you.

Dear _____,

Dear _____,

CULTIVATING DIVINE MOTHER AND FATHER ENERGY

By stepping out of the role of child with your parents and embodying the energy of your divine inner mother or father, you can develop an integrated capacity to care for yourself and provide self-nurturing. Here you will reflect on what you want to feel, hear, and experience most from a wise inner parent and see how you might offer this to yourself.

Did you feel seen and understood by your parents, or misunderstood and alone?

....

....

....

....

....

Your divine inner parent: *Take a moment to listen to your inner child, to their needs, fears, and feelings. What are they saying? If you could speak to "little you" back then, what would you say to make them feel seen, understood, and valued?*

....

....

....

....

....

Did you feel like you were responsible for your parents' emotions or well-being when you were a child? Did you feel like the caretaker rather than the child?

_____

_____

_____

_____

_____

_____

Your divine inner parent: *Remember you do not have to do everything on your own. Is there an area in your life that could use some softening, or where you can allow others to support you?*

_____

_____

_____

_____

_____

_____

Did you feel like you were protected by your parents or often left to fend for yourself? Were your parents reliable, or did you often feel that they did not come through for you?

....
....
....
....
....
....
....

Your divine inner parent: *How can you tap into your own protective energy? Is there a fierce boundary you can set or a personal goal you can follow through on?*

....
....
....
....
....
....
....

Did you feel safe to express yourself as a child? Or were you expected to behave a certain way that made you feel like something about you wasn't acceptable?

....

....

....

....

....

....

....

Your divine inner parent: *Is there something that you were taught was "unacceptable" that you can give yourself permission to do or be? (For example, taking time to rest, feeling sad or angry, making mistakes, etc.)*

....

....

....

....

....

....

....

Is there a specific relationship or area in your life that requires your divine inner-parent energy and attention right now?

_____

_____

_____

_____

_____

_____

_____

Were you allowed to be playful as a child or to make mistakes? Or were you often striving, overachieving, or attempting to be perfect?

_____

_____

_____

_____

_____

_____

_____

_____

Did you feel you had to earn attention and love from your parents by behaving a certain way?

....
....
....
....
....
....
....
....

What behaviors were rewarded and what parts of yourself did you feel you had to suppress?

....
....
....
....
....
....
....
....

Forgiveness is the road to internal freedom.
It widens our capacity to open ourselves to love
again, to trust ourselves, and to experience the
depth and beauty that life has to offer.

7

FINDING FREEDOM
THROUGH
FORGIVENESS

SO OFTEN IN THE SPIRITUAL AND PERSONAL GROWTH realms, we're told that to heal we must forgive. We may interpret this as needing to be warm or offer a second chance to whomever has caused us pain. The truth of forgiveness is that it's an internal process, meant to release you from your own suffering. Forgiveness has very little to do with the other person. It doesn't mean we aren't allowed to have boundaries or end a relationship for good. There may also be times where forgiveness feels unreachable, and in these scenarios, we can look toward acceptance. Acceptance is important because regardless of whether we feel ready to forgive, to liberate ourselves from any lingering resentment, anger, and suffering, we must accept our circumstances and our past.

Acceptance is the doorway to freedom. It is the key to releasing yourself from reliving the event. Most important, it is taking back your power and no longer allowing those who hurt you to take up residence in your mind.

The process of forgiveness and acceptance cannot be rushed. Whatever emotions arise for you—sadness, anger—allow yourself the space to experience your feelings. In this section, you'll have an opportunity to explore any of your unhealed relationships from the past that need completion, as well as learn rituals and practices for self-forgiveness.

EXPLORING YOUR UNHEALED
RELATIONSHIPS

You can repeat the following process with as many of your past relationships as feels necessary. As with all healing practices regarding another
person, this work is for you, not for them. You do not need to share any
of this with the actual person if they are from your past.

Write down a list of anyone you feel incomplete with (for example,
family, teachers, friends, colleagues, etc.). Maybe you had a "bad
ending," harbor anger toward them, hold resentment toward them, or
your relationship with them feels unhealed.

From your list, choose one person that feels the most "charged" energetically for you. Write the reasons you may be angry, hurt, or resentful using the following sentence stems. You can repeat this with the other people on your list when you are ready.

I'm angry at you because:

I'm feeling hurt because:

I feel resentful because:

I benefit from holding on to my anger and pain toward you because:

If I were to release you from the anger/pain/resentment I've held on to, I would experience:

SELF-FORGIVENESS

Often the person we need to forgive most is *ourselves*. It's painful to hold ourselves in blame and shame, or to replay past events in our mind and wonder if it was all our fault or if we should have done something differently. Each of us has a unique path to our own healing, and every experience, heartache, mistake, and lesson you have gathered holds meaning for you now. Be grateful to your past selves for carrying you to this point. Have compassion and reverence for the person you were then, doing your best with the conditioning and awareness you had at the time.

Now you are creating a bright new future full of possibilities. So long as you believe you don't deserve to have more because of your past mistakes, you will remain stuck. The next few sentence stems and rituals are designed to help you become open to self-forgiveness and invite you to step fully into a new chapter where you embody the knowing that you are whole and worthy of the kind of life your heart desires most.

I blame myself for:

....

....

....

....

....

....

Something I wish I had done differently is:

....

....

....

....

....

....

....

....

I acknowledge now that I was doing my best with the tools I had.
I have compassion for everything I was going through at the time,
which was (describe your state of mind, environment, stresses you
were dealing with back then):

....

....

....

....

....

....

....

....

....

I honor myself for (describe your growth and the positive choices you made that led you here):

....
....
....
....
....
....
....
....

If I were to forgive myself for my past choices and mistakes, my life would improve in these ways:

....
....
....
....
....
....
....
....
....

FREE-JOURNAL

Write about any feelings, strong emotions, or thoughts this process has brought up for you. Allow yourself to express and release whatever has come to the surface—let it flow through you and onto the page.

SELF-FORGIVENESS TEA RITUAL

Heart Healing: *rose or hawthorn tea*

Heart Opening and Calming: *rose or chamomile tea*

If you cannot find or are not drawn to the herbal teas suggested here, you can intuitively choose something else that works for you. Even a simple store-bought loose-leaf or bagged tea is perfectly fine. Remember what matters most in these healing practices is the act of ritual.

1. **Step into Ceremony:** Make yourself a cup of rose, chamomile, hawthorn, or other tea of your choice. Go to your ritual spot or find a quiet space in your home to sit with your tea and light a candle.

2. **Sit in Presence and Gratitude:** Hold the warm mug of tea in your hands and thank the flowers and the water for their medicine. As you sip your tea, take a moment to appreciate yourself for all that you have been through and all the experiences that have brought you to this precious moment in time.

3. **Bathe in Self-Love:** Set down your tea, place both hands on your heart, and close your eyes. Visualize your inner child, your inner teenager, your past selves, the most potent experiences that have imprinted on you up until now. In your mind or out loud, say, "I see you, I love you, I forgive you, I accept you."

4. **Honor Your Past Experiences:** Thank all versions of yourself for having the courage to heal and imagine your entire body filling with crystal-clear blue water, starting at the bottom of your feet, all the way through your body, and pouring out of the crown of your head.

5. **Release the Past:** As the crystal-clear water cleanses your body and spirit, imagine a golden light filling your being and emanating from your body. Open your eyes and continue to enjoy your tea with the intention of releasing yourself from past guilt and stepping into self-love and acceptance.

Choose a word or two that encapsulates your intention for this ritual (for example: self-love, trust, healing).

Are there any beliefs or patterns you're ready to release?

ACCEPT AND RELEASE MOON RITUAL

New Moon: On the eve or day of a new moon, go for a walk and gather items from nature that represent the journey you are on. Like many nature rituals, allow this to be intuitive. The symbology you assign to what you gather is completely up to you. Let your creativity rather than your logical mind guide you. These items should be things that you can eventually give back to the earth, bury, or toss in the ocean. Do not use anything that isn't organic and biodegradable and sustainable. Flowers, leaves, pine cones, rocks, or crystals are wonderful choices.

Waxing Moon: As the full moon approaches, spend some time tuning in and, as you place each item on your altar, consider what each represents and where you are in your current journey. You can also add your letter to your parents or any other items that may represent the relationship you're working on healing. If you are going through a breakup or a divorce, it's possible you will feel called to place certain items that represent your relationship or that you received as a gift.

Full Moon: Slowly release each item on your altar. You may wish to safely burn a letter or a photo. If the item belongs in nature, you can return it. If it is something that needs to be donated or gifted, make a plan for this. Only release an item that you feel truly ready to let go of.

Healing is not a call to change the essence of who you are, but to let down your walls and return to the truth of your essence.

8

TRANSFORMING
YOUR RELATIONSHIP
PATTERNS

WHEN WE THINK OF HEALING OUR RELATIONSHIP patterns, we might believe we are meant to "break" or "get rid of" them entirely. What we are actually doing is increasing our awareness of our role in them and *transforming the energy* to reach greater heights of intimacy, connection, safety, and love. The beautiful thing is, just as there is a shadow expression of our patterns, there is also a healthy expression. To create change, however, we cannot view our behaviors through a judgmental lens. This only induces shame and self-blame. Instead, we want to find a place of understanding and self-compassion for how that pattern has served us up until now and then make room for a new expression.

No matter how much inner work we do, new patterns or realizations will emerge so long as we are engaged in partnership with another human being. Rather than trying to arrive at a finish line, embrace relationship as a spiritual path of continual learning and self-discovery.

There's a spectrum to everything, and it's an oversimplification to think that we should enter a relationship only with someone who is "secure" or that somehow our own part in a pattern will dissolve so long as all our needs are met. The truth is, we learn and grow in partnership by coming up against those hard-to-look-at places. We heal together when we recognize the pattern and choose to move toward a more mature and healthy way of relating despite our instinct to put up walls or fall back into an old dance. Rather than looking for the perfect partner or trying to be perfect ourselves, we can look for traits like honesty, willingness to lean in when things are hard, and the courage to be vulnerable or apologize. These are the kinds of traits that healthy long-term couples possess, but I assure you none of them have reached perfection.

To begin to unravel the origin of our patterns, we must first take a closer look at the very first relationship we have in life, the relationship we have with our parents. This is where we learned everything we know about love, connection, and safety.

In this section, you're going to learn to identify some of your earliest conditioning, and how this has formed some of your beliefs and your unique relationship patterns. Then you will have an opportunity to see how you are playing out that pattern, take full responsibility for it, and commit to showing up as a more empowered, self-aware version of yourself.

COMMON RELATIONSHIP PATTERNS

Self-abandoning

Avoiding intimacy

Chasing unavailable or unsafe love

People pleasing

Withholding our truth

Shape-shifting to be who others want us to be

Moving too quickly without qualifying someone

Switching between "unsafe" and "safe" partners

Volatile conflicts and fighting

Leaving before being left

Staying in relationships out of guilt

Becoming a caretaker in relationship
(embodying the role of parent)

Underfunctioning in relationship
(embodying the role of dependent)

EXPLORING YOUR CONDITIONING
AROUND LOVE

What did you observe from your parents' relationship? Were they together, married, divorced? If you had a single parent, what did you notice about how they engaged in dating and romantic relationships?

....

....

....

....

....

....

What was your mother's attitude toward men?

....

....

....

....

....

....

....

What was your mother's attitude toward women?

....
....
....
....
....
....

What was your father's attitude toward women?

....
....
....
....
....
....

What was your father's attitude toward men?

....
....
....
....
....
....

What was your mother and father's attitude toward sexuality? Was it openly discussed in your home? How so?

....
....
....
....
....
....
....
....

Was there physical affection, words of affirmation, and expression of love in your home growing up?

....
....
....
....
....
....
....
....

How did your parents navigate conflict? (For example, with open communication, calmness, anger, explosive behavior, blaming or shaming, withholding, denying, etc.)

....

....

....

....

....

....

....

Did they model repair after conflict or not? If so, what did that look like? (For example, shutting down, yelling, dismissing, avoiding, or taking responsibility, respectfulness, genuine apologies, giving space, etc.)

....

....

....

....

....

....

....

Did you feel you could trust your parents consistently to do what they said they would do? Why or why not?

What were your biggest complaints about how your parents showed up when you were a child?

What are your favorite memories from childhood involving a parent or caregiver?

....

....

....

....

....

....

....

....

Reflect on the journaling you did in chapter 6. What were some of your favorite and least favorite qualities in your parents or caregiver?

....

....

....

....

....

....

....

....

EXPLORING YOUR RELATIONSHIPS

What were your earliest beliefs around marriage and love, and what are they now? How have they changed over time?

_____

_____

_____

_____

_____

_____

_____

What were your earliest thoughts or beliefs about sex and intimacy?

_____

_____

_____

_____

_____

_____

_____

How do you express love or affection within your relationships?

Do you find it difficult or easy to be vulnerable with a partner? What does establishing trust with them look like?

In your most recent romantic relationships, what were your biggest complaints about your partners?

_____

_____

_____

_____

_____

_____

_____

_____

What are your favorite memories or experiences you've shared with past or present partners?

_____

_____

_____

_____

_____

_____

_____

_____

_____

What are the qualities that you are most drawn to in your partners?

Do you see any similar themes between what you valued as a child
from a caregiver and what you value now in current partners?

Are there any overlaps with some of the negative qualities in your parents and your current or past partners?

Are there any qualities you have rejected in a partner that you may also reject in yourself?

CONNECTING THE PAST AND PRESENT

What similar themes did you discover? Focus on the overall emotional tone, meaning the core of what you felt in both your relationships with a romantic partner and with your parents or caregivers growing up.

For example, "In my romantic relationships I've always felt misunderstood. When I was growing up, I never felt like my parents understood me. In my childhood, I always enjoyed adventure with my parents, but they were emotionally unavailable. In my romantic relationships, I'm drawn to people who are exciting and adventurous but emotionally unavailable."

The following sentence stems are designed to help you identify where you may be holding on to any self-sabotaging beliefs from your earliest conditioning, or whether an unresolved pain or need from the past is playing out in your present relationships. Go as deep as you can with each of your responses.

My past romantic partners were always:

....

....

....

....

....

....

My past romantic partners never:

Something I always wanted to hear from my romantic partner is:

Something I always wanted my romantic partner to do for me is:

My mother or father was always:

My mother or father was never:

Something I always wanted to hear from my mother or father is:

Something I always wanted my mother or father to do for me is:

....
....
....
....
....
....
....
....
....

In all of my past relationships, I consistently felt:

....
....
....
....
....
....
....
....
....
....

In my past relationships, my response to conflict was usually to (pursue, chase, avoid, withdraw, hide, hold back, shut down, assume the worst, fight, etc.):

....

....

....

....

....

....

....

In my past relationships, I would end or repair the conflict by:

....

....

....

....

....

....

....

....

....

In the space below, list all of your romantic relationships. Include how long they each lasted, how they each ended, and the overall tone of each relationship.

FINDING THE THEMES

If you could pull out three core emotional themes and make a sentence out of them, what would they be? For example, "In all of my romantic relationships, I consistently felt abandoned," or "In all of my romantic relationships, I always felt like I was walking on eggshells."

Core theme 1:

....

....

....

Core theme 2:

....

....

....

Core theme 3:

....

....

....

What came up for you in this chapter?

Was there anything that surprised you?

BEGINNING TO SHIFT THE PATTERN'S ENERGY

After identifying some of your core themes or patterns, if you are feeling a sense of overwhelm or shame, I encourage you to carry on to the next chapter. The prompts and practices that follow will help ground you in self-compassion and love so you can begin to transform the shadow energy of a pattern into a higher frequency of expression.

Rather than looking to extinguish this part of you, I invite you to look at this journey as a path to embodying your most authentic self that is secure, confident, and trusts in your own worth. While awareness of a pattern doesn't erase it, what we can do is be mindful in triggering moments, center ourselves, and do our best to act from the present rather than from our wound. We will never get it right one hundred percent of the time, so give yourself grace and make space for lasting change.

A behavior that was serving me back then is:

....

....

....

....

....

....

....

That behavior is no longer serving me now because:

Something I'm committed to shifting in my relationship patterns is:

Deepening in self-awareness and transforming
our patterns is possible only with equal
amounts of self-compassion and acceptance.

9

SHADOW WORK
AND
SELF-COMPASSION

ONE OF THE REASONS WE MAY HESITATE TO LOOK INWARD is the guilt and shame that can follow when we see the role we've played in our own relationship breakdowns and painful experiences. Shining a light on our own shadow tendencies takes immense courage. Although it isn't easy to be accountable for the ways we avoid intimacy, lash out from our wounded inner child, or act from our shadow side, it's intensely liberating. By lifting the veil and seeing ourselves more clearly, we heal our relationship to ourselves and to others.

Whatever we deny and reject in ourselves doesn't vanish, it simply grows quietly underneath the surface and bubbles out at the most inopportune times, namely in our relationships. When we don't give ourselves permission to express these parts of ourselves, we end up acting out, pushing love away, or losing trust in ourselves. Rest assured that no human being on the planet has a perfect record. We are all responsible for hurting others unintentionally, behaving in ways we aren't proud of, or saying the "wrong" thing. All we can do is learn from our history and heal these wounds so that a more authentic expression of our feelings, fears, and vulnerabilities can be revealed.

We act out or defend because somewhere along the way we learned it wasn't safe to show others who we really are. As a little girl, I was incredibly sensitive and compassionate. As I began to endure traumas, experienced ruptures in my bond with my mother through abandonment and mental health challenges, and entered the foster system, I became hardened and guarded. No one could get through to me; I was in total self-protection mode. If I was hurting, I wouldn't let it show; instead I would project anger as a way of appearing "tough" so that I didn't get hurt or, even worse, have to feel the pain and disappointment of being let down by another person I trusted. My journey has been one of de-armoring my heart and returning to my innate sensitivity and compassionate essence. I see the hurt little girl that needed to be strong, and now I can be strong yet open, boundaried but not walled, honest but not harsh.

Accountability, shadow work, and self-compassion is the medicine that led me along my healing path and that you will work with in this chapter. Trust that the more honest you allow yourself to be, the more potential you have to unlock healing and the truth of who you are. Whatever you uncover in this chapter, know that you are worthy of having the kind of life and relationships your heart craves. The purpose of doing shadow work is not to punish ourselves for our mistakes, but to usher us into a greater sense of awareness and make way for true self-acceptance.

SHINING A LIGHT WITHIN

Draw on your journal responses from chapter 8 for this section. Reflect on your relationship patterns and the ways you may have acted out in conflict. Consider the similarities between your childhood experiences and your romantic partnerships.

When you are in relationship, what's the most common negative emotion you tend to experience? (For example, anger, jealousy, shame, insecurity, etc.)

....

....

....

....

....

....

How does this emotion serve as protection for you?

....

....

....

....

....

....

If you were to express the emotion or fear that's living underneath that emotional response, what would you say? (For example, "I'm afraid of being left," or "I'm scared to be taken advantage of.")

What do you wish people saw in you?

What are you afraid people see in you?

What do people assume about you that feels hurtful?

What is an aspect of your personality or character that you judge the most?

What are you afraid that aspect of your personality or character means about you?

What is something you've been judged or criticized for in the past?

What about this particular judgment or criticism stung the most for you?

Do you see any truth to this judgment or criticism?

When you make a mistake, feel embarrassed, or feel put on the spot, what is your instinctual reaction? (For example, blame, defending, denying, lashing out, etc.)

How would you like to respond instead?

OPEN MY HEART CACAO

Cacao has long been cherished and used ceremonially as a sacred medicine by Central and South American cultures for its heart-opening properties. When you are feeling defensive or self-critical, try this simple heart-opening ritual.

1 cup hot milk of choice or boiled water

1 tablespoon cacao powder

1 tablespoon honey or maple syrup

½ teaspoon vanilla extract

Pinch of cinnamon

Pinch of sea salt

Heat the milk or water in a mug, then carefully mix in the cacao powder, honey, vanilla, cinnamon, and sea salt, infusing love into your cup. When your drink is ready, sit quietly and with each sip envision any walls or fears slowly beginning to dissolve.

Visualize a beautiful pink mist coming from your heart and permeating your entire body. As you allow the loving intention of this moment to soften you, connect back to the deepest part of yourself that is innocent and tender. It is in our capacity to remember our softness so that we grow in our capacity to be graceful with others.

COMPASSIONATE SELF-AWARENESS

Complete the following sentence stems.

Sometimes when I'm overwhelmed by my feelings, I:

....

....

....

....

....

....

....

....

When I'm hurt, I react by:

....

....

....

....

....

....

....

....

When I'm angry, I react by:

If I were to show people who I really am, they would:

I'm afraid to be vulnerable with others because:

I'm afraid to express my anger with others because:

If I were to be fully expressed, I would:

If I were to love and accept myself, I would:

If I were to bring more awareness to my relationships, I would:

_____

_____

_____

_____

_____

_____

_____

_____

_____

If I speak my truth and bring more honesty and vulnerability to my relationships, my life will improve in the following ways:

_____

_____

_____

_____

_____

_____

_____

_____

_____

Five things I am proud of myself for:

1.

2.

3.

4.

5.

SOFTENING YOUR INTERNAL DIALOGUE

How we speak to ourselves matters. Moment to moment, bring compassion to your process and allow your inner awareness to guide you. If you slip into a familiar habitual response when emotions are high, rather than being hard on yourself, take a pause and a few breaths and try to soften your inner dialogue. You can practice this by completing the following sentences:

Even though sometimes I _____, I am still a good person.

Even though sometimes I feel _____, I am worthy of love.

Even though sometimes I judge myself for _____ _____, I know that underneath that is _____ _____.

Even though I have made mistakes in the past, I celebrate myself for _____.

As I embark on my healing journey, I am committed to seeing myself as _____.

SELF-COMPASSION NATURE ALTAR RITUAL

When you look at the rhythms of the earth, you see that nature has room for both dark and light, death and rebirth, bloom and decay. In the same way, all that lives inside of you has a right to exist. Each piece of the altar you will build represents a part of you that you are bringing forward and viewing through a lens of compassion. It will also represent elements (earth, water, fire, air) or supportive influences you wish to call into your life. For example, you may choose an item in the center that represents you, and circle it with items from nature that represent the community you'd like to surround you.

The intention in building a nature altar is multifaceted: It is a way for you to connect with Spirit, nature, and yourself and to invite slowness and beauty into your experience. Rituals such as these are meant to be meditative in nature and uplift your entire being.

To Begin

Gather flowers, leaves, pine cones, seeds, nuts, fruit, or other organic items. Choose a spot outside to build your nature altar, perhaps on a beach, in a forest, by a river, or somewhere in your own yard if you have access to outdoor space. Be mindful of how this may impact other creatures living in the area and do not use any items that may hurt or harm the environment or animals if left behind.

Creating Your Nature Altar

Intuitively place your objects in a circular fashion. There's no right or wrong way to make a nature altar. Begin by creating a centerpiece, perhaps with a flower or something beautiful, and build out from the middle. You may say a prayer or intention of compassion and self-acceptance as you place each item, imagining any pain or shame you feel toward your past selves transforming into gratitude, into peace. You are here because of all the versions of you that have come before, because of your light and your shadow. Allow whatever wants to come up to flow through you in this process.

Fear feels urgent and may cause us to push
love away. Intuition may ask us to do hard
things, but it will always move us toward
what serves our highest good.

10

LEARNING TO
TRUST YOURSELF

IN OUR CHAOTIC WORLD, LEARNING HOW TO SLOW DOWN
and listen to our bodies and intuition is a skill that requires practice
and patience. It's not enough to simply say "trust your heart" or "trust
your body," because many of us may be clouded by our past experiences
and traumas. This can lead us to assume the worst in others, craft stories, or distance ourselves from what we truly want: love and connection. To trust our bodies and create a clean line of communication with
our intuition, we must be aware of our internalized fears or defenses.

Many of us leave our bodies during an experience of physical or
emotional boundary violation to self-protect. This leads us to rely on
logic and the mind to make decisions, moving us further and further
away from our body's wisdom. When we are solely in our heads, we
might believe our emotions need to make sense to be valid, or we might
make decisions that are practical but don't fulfill us on a soul level.
With any relationship, we need a strong connection to this internal
guidance to know what boundaries to set, when to lean in, and when
to walk away.

In this chapter, you're going to have an opportunity to connect
more deeply to your body by tuning in to your sensations and identifying the difference between a false alarm and your intuition. As you
return to your body, you will discover how to create your life from a
place of self-trust. When mind and body are connected, rather than
acting on fear or the incessant mind-chatter generated from the past,
you will be able to act from a grounded place.

WHEN IN TUNE WITH OUR BODIES, WE CAN IDENTIFY . . .

Our energetic and physical limits

What feels good and what doesn't

When we need slowness, support, space,
or connection

Cues from our partners in relationship

WHEN MIND AND BODY ARE CONNECTED, WE CAN . . .

Make decisions that align with
our lives as a whole

Move through emotions so they
don't manifest into physical illness

Have deeper access to our motivations,
triggers, desires, and needs

Hold ourselves through challenging moments

Express ourselves maturely in relationship

THE BODY SCAN RITUAL

How often do you ignore your body's hunger signals, thirst signals, or the need to pee? This ritual will help you reconnect to your body while practicing listening and responding to what is happening within. Make a habit of doing this ritual once or twice daily for a week, when you wake up, right before bed, or midday. Notice how you begin to hear and recognize your bodily sensations and feelings more clearly over time. This process doesn't have to result in a profound insight; simply bringing yourself more into your body is a gift.

1. Sit comfortably in a quiet place. Gently breathe and feel your lungs inhale and exhale. Place a hand on your belly or heart and give thanks to your body for all the work it does to give you life, day in and day out.

2. Now, bring your awareness to the bottom of your feet. Notice how it feels to be connected to the ground beneath you. Slowly make your way up your body, tuning in to each sensation in your legs, thighs, bottom, back, belly, chest, heart, throat, face, and the crown of your head.

3. With each moment of awareness, notice what sensations you are experiencing (cold, hot, tension, pain, tingling, constriction, etc.). With each breath, notice what kind of emotions you feel (calm, anxiety, anger, excitement, etc.).

4. Next, see if you can identify where in your body you are experiencing each sensation and emotion. Ask your body, "What do I need right now?"

In the space below, write anything that came up for you during this ritual. Was it easy or difficult to be with the sensations in your body? Describe your experience.

THE MIND-BODY CONNECTION

Complete the following sentence stems. *Remember, write whatever thoughts or feelings come to mind first and until you are empty.*

I'm afraid to be in my body because:

....

....

....

....

....

I'm grateful for my body because:

....

....

....

....

I make decisions from my head when:

....

....

....

....

I make decisions from my body when:

Intuition is:

My body is:

THE DIFFERENCE BETWEEN
FEAR AND INTUITION

FEAR LOOKS LIKE . . .

Creating an elaborate story of the future

Making assumptions about someone's intentions

Reacting before taking a moment to pause and reflect

A sensation of urgency that requires immediate action

INTUITION LOOKS LIKE . . .

A subtle inner knowing

A light whisper rather than a frantic demand

An instinctual sensation rather than a story

Recall a time when you experienced clarity of intuition:

....

....

....

....

....

What did it feel like in your body? What sensations were there? Where in your body was your intuition located?

....

....

....

....

....

....

....

....

Recall a time where you ignored your intuition:

....

....

....

....

....

....

....

....

....

Did you experience a moment of clarity afterward, and what did you do with that information?

....

....

....

....

....

....

....

....

After ignoring your intuition, did you trust yourself? What was that like for you?

....

....

....

....

....

....

....

....

....

Recall a time in a past relationship where you thought you had an intuition about something but later realized that it was coming from fear. What was that like for you?

....

....

....

....

....

....

....

....

Recall a time when you made a decision purely from your head or logic within a relationship. How did that impact you?

....

....

....

....

....

....

....

....

....

....

Do you recall feelings that arose when you were in that decision-making process? What was your response? (For example, stuffing down, distracting, ignoring your feelings/sensations, etc.)

Describe what anger feels like as a sensation in your body. (Is it hot or cold, heavy or light? Where is it located in your body? Does it have a color or a shape?)

Describe what sadness feels like as a sensation in your body. (Is it hot or cold, heavy or light? Where is it located in your body? Does it have a color or a shape?)

....

....

....

....

....

....

....

What are some practices you enjoy that bring you into your body when you're feeling stuck in your head? (For example, yoga, dance, breathwork, massage, walks, stretching, etc.)

....

....

....

....

....

....

....

....

ENHANCING YOUR INTUITION

WAYS TO TAP INTO YOUR INTUITION

Do body scans daily

Spend time in nature without distractions

Create a journaling practice

Eat grounding foods like root veggies, potatoes, squash

Limit stimulant intake (coffee/excess media)

Drink soothing and calming teas

Movement and exercise

How will your life improve if you begin to practice being in your
body and trusting your intuition more?

....

....

....

....

....

....

....

....

....

In what ways will you commit to tuning in to your body? How will you carve out time for just "being" so you can hear your inner voice more clearly?

Our relationships always reflect our
values, consciously or unconsciously.
When we know what guides us,
we have the power to choose our
relationships with intention.

11

DISCOVER
THE VALUES THAT
LEAD YOU

OUR CORE VALUES ARE WHAT GUIDE OUR CHOICES IN all areas of life. Either consciously or unconsciously, what we value determines the kind of relationships we have. The challenge is, many of us weren't taught how to examine or define our core values. So, instead of carefully choosing our relationships, we may find ourselves falling into them.

Knowing our values is vital to qualifying a partner, to see if we are aligned spiritually and emotionally. Surprisingly, the ways we tend to swing out of balance in our relationships is also an indicator of what we value *most*.

Let me share a little example with you. Generosity and abundance are two very important values to me. My friends know that when they come to my home, they will be well fed and provided for and that I love to care for people in this way! While I am more likely to want to give everything away for free, my husband is more financially mindful. At times, this has bothered me, just as my attitude of "it will always come back to us" seems a little too impractical for his taste. While my husband is indeed a very generous man, his core values of integrity and responsibility sit near the top of his own values hierarchy.

Often, we want our partner to share every single core value we have, and we look for evidence that we're not perfectly matched when this doesn't align. In some cases, when our partner doesn't have the same hierarchy of values as we do, this is a gift. My husband may lean into his relationship to abundance by being married to me, while I get to strengthen my relationship to financial responsibility. And when my core value of generosity slips too far into caretaker mode, my husband may help bring this imbalance into my awareness. We do these things for each other and for ourselves as a celebration of our love and the growth that it brings us. In every relationship there are going to be core values that we absolutely must share in common at the same level of priority, and some we may not value in the same way that bring polarity and give us an opportunity to grow.

You don't have to value all the same things, practice the same spiritual routines, or share all your hobbies in common to experience a conscious relationship. What's most important is sharing mutual respect, willingness, curiosity, chemistry, trust, and the values that guide your lives.

Unrealistic expectations or seeking to have everything in common with a partner can make it impossible for anyone to live up to our standards. It takes an honest relationship with ourselves to recognize if what we're asking for from a partner stems from a healthy place or a wounded place. Only when we can recognize the difference can we experience true fulfillment and mature partnership.

Throughout this journal you have discovered the common traits, qualities, and emotional themes within your past relationships. You will now have a chance to pull from some of those exercises to help you get crystal clear on what your core values are and how to embody them in your everyday life.

Being safe to express yourself and your emotions

Open and honest communication

Having similar and different interests and values

You won't meet each other's needs one hundred percent
of the time

You will have challenges and conflict

Your healing work will always be in progress

You and your partner will continue to change

Having a rich, fulfilling love beyond the honeymoon phase

DISCOVER YOUR CORE VALUES

We can learn about our core values by reflecting on our past romantic relationships. What was it that attracted you to that person? What qualities did you admire in them? What aspects of the relationship were you most excited about?

At times, our core values may have swung out of balance when we prioritized adventure or sexual passion over safety and respect. While all core values are important, we need to identify which ones are nonnegotiable, which are nice to have, and which are necessary additions but won't be enough to create a mature and loving partnership on their own. This begins by defining which values we've inherited from others or our family conditioning and claiming the values that are truly ours.

The following list of core values is not complete; it is meant to give you just an overview of some of the many that exist.

Abundance	Community	Inspiration
Acceptance	Companionship	Integrity
Accountability	Contribution	Optimism
Acknowledgment	Creativity	Presence
Adventure	Family	Punctuality
Affection	Freedom	Purpose
Appreciation	Friendship	Quality Time
Authenticity	Fun	Recognition
Autonomy	Generosity	Reliability
Awareness	Gifts	Religion and Faith
Balance	Gratitude	Respect
Beauty	Growth	Risk-taking
Belonging	Harmony	Safety
Candor	Health	Security
Challenge	Honesty	Self-acceptance
Change	Hope	Self-awareness
Choice	Humility	Self-expression
Cleanliness	Humor	Self-respect
Closeness	Inclusion	Sensitivity
Collaboration	Independence	Sensuality
Commitment	Innovation	Spirituality

What core values did your parents model when you were growing up?
What were you raised to value?

_____

_____

_____

_____

_____

What core values, if any, did your parents have that you don't?

_____

_____

_____

_____

_____

What core values do you recognize you were prioritizing in some of
your past relationships?

_____

_____

_____

_____

_____

If you had to choose five core values that matter most to you, what would they be?

1. ....

2. ....

3. ....

4. ....

5. ....

Why did you choose these core values in particular? What do they mean to you?

....

....

....

....

....

....

What core values do you feel you absolutely have to have in a partner and why?

....

....

....

....

....

What would it mean if your partner didn't have all these core values? What would happen?

....

....

....

....

....

Reflect on a time when you ignored your core values. How did that turn out?

....

....

....

....

....

In the past, what expectations have you placed on a partner that you now realize came from a wound and not your mature adult self?

....

....

....

....

....

Are there any areas within your relationships where you could offer more room for differences or imperfection?

....

....

....

....

....

....

What are some core values you admire in others or want in a partner that you may not yet embody?

....

....

....

....

....

....

EMBODYING YOUR CORE VALUES

Living our values is a daily practice. Reflect back on your list of top five core values. Within each of the major areas of your life, consider if you are living in alignment with each of these values, and if not, brainstorm ways you can embody your core values more day to day. For example, if you value adventure, where in your life might you be missing this? If you value commitment, are you honoring your commitments to yourself and others in each area of your life? And if not, how can you embody this value more?

ROMANTIC RELATIONSHIP

Top Core Values	*Nice-to-Have Values*	*Values I Want to Grow Into*

FAMILY

*Top Core
Values*

*Nice-to-Have
Values*

*Values I Want
to Grow Into*

WORK

*Top Core
Values*

*Nice-to-Have
Values*

*Values I Want
to Grow Into*

FRIENDSHIPS AND COMMUNITY

Top Core Values	*Nice-to-Have Values*	*Values I Want to Grow Into*

SPIRITUALITY

Top Core Values	*Nice-to-Have Values*	*Values I Want to Grow Into*

SELF

Top Core Values	Nice-to-Have Values	Values I Want to Grow Into

WEALTH

Top Core Values	Nice-to-Have Values	Values I Want to Grow Into

Heart-led boundaries serve as a
how-to manual on how to be in a healthy
relationship with yourself and others.

12

SET HEART-LED
BOUNDARIES

AT THEIR HEART, BOUNDARIES REFLECT OUR RELATION-
ship to self and our commitment to honesty. There are times when our
boundaries may need to be fierce and serve to close doors or draw a
line in the sand when something in a relationship is out of alignment.
Boundaries are not meant to be walls to keep others at arm's length,
but rather a way to strengthen our relationships and maintain healthy
connections with others.

When we are in tune with our bodies and our own needs on a spiritual, mental, emotional, material, and physical level, living in authenticity becomes nearly effortless. Authenticity is the result of having
clear boundaries with ourselves and others that reflect what we want to
experience in every area of our lives, be that at work, at home, or with
our families.

FIVE TYPES OF BOUNDARIES

Physical: Your body and personal space

Material: Physical items and personal belongings

Mental: Your thoughts, sense of self, values, and opinions

Spiritual: Your spiritual practices, belief systems,
life philosophies, and karmic path

Emotional: Separating our emotions from others,
knowing the difference between what we are feeling
and someone else's experience

YOUR BOUNDARY SIGNATURES

Within different relationship dynamics, we may experience different boundary challenges. For example, if you had a particularly challenging history with your mother or with female friends in school, you may find that your *boundary signature* (porous, rigid, or healthy) shifts around women who represent those archetypes from your history, whereas in other relationships, you find boundary-setting less confronting. In this section you will reflect on your boundary signature within each area of your life.

POROUS

Struggles to say no

Easily influenced by others

Feels burnt out, bitter, and resentful

Takes on others' problems

Acts from fear of rejection and abandonment

Has caretaker or rescuer energy

Relies on external validation

Sees boundaries as mean

RIGID

Stubborn and not open to any influence

Defensive rather than curious

Uses boundaries to shield or guard the heart

Uses pride to shield emotional vulnerability

Is unwilling to collaborate

Is more self-centered than relational

HEALTHY

Can be firm or flexible when necessary

Respects others' boundaries

Trusts in the body and inner voice

Consciously chooses how to respond to
opinions and feedback

Holds space for others' emotions
without rescuing or caretaking

Can say no, even if that means feeling some guilt

Shares personal information without
under- or oversharing

Communicates boundaries clearly and directly

Uses boundaries to create healthier relationships

Knows self and communicates needs

What boundary signature do you resonate most with overall?

What is your boundary signature in romantic relationships and how has this signature impacted your relationships?

What is your boundary signature in platonic friendships? How has this signature impacted your relationships?

When you were a child, were boundaries respected in your family system? Describe how or how not:

Does your signature change with men versus women? If so, why do you think that is?

What is your boundary signature with those you respect, admire, or consider authority figures? Describe what you think drives this:

Recall a time in your past when you knew you needed to set a boundary, but didn't out of anxiety or fear:

_____
_____
_____
_____
_____
_____
_____
_____
_____

What were you afraid would happen?

_____
_____
_____
_____
_____
_____
_____
_____
_____

When you need to set a boundary with someone, how does it feel in your body? What are the signs that you need to speak up or make a change?

When you ignore a boundary or commitment you've made to yourself, how does it feel in your body? How does it impact you? (For example, sleep changes, more anxiety, etc.)

FINDING YOUR BALANCE

Sometimes when we're learning how to set boundaries in a healthy way, it might take time for us to find the right balance. If setting boundaries is typically difficult, it will feel incredibly foreign to us. We may unintentionally come off as if we are making demands or being accusatory. Our challenge is to self-soothe the anxiety or nervousness that is hiding underneath this over-expression so that we can state our needs in a calm and clear way. On the other hand, if we've been guarded and walled, our work is to soften and give others a chance to meet us where we want to be met rather than closing up shop before any communication or attempts to repair have been made.

The area in which you are presently being asked to grow beyond a comfortable habit or pattern is called your *growth edge*. In essence, it's the inner work you're being called to most at this time.

What do you think your growth edge is in the realm of boundaries currently? (For example, setting boundaries more gently or more firmly, honoring the boundaries you set for yourself, letting people in more, etc.)

Reflect on the five types of boundaries (physical, material, mental, spiritual, emotional). Are there any areas where you could have healthier boundaries?

How do you imagine your life improving when you make these shifts toward having healthier boundaries?

COMMUNICATING BOUNDARIES

WHEN EXPRESSING BOUNDARIES . . .

Know Your Intention

Do you want more connection, to shift the relationship dynamic, to change a behavior?

Be Direct

Be clear about what you need, rather than focusing on blame. Use "I" statements rather than "you," which can feel accusatory.

Give Mutual Respect

Remember this is a two-way street. Follow the boundaries you set for yourself and respect others' boundaries.

Be Patient

You may meet some initial resistance; sometimes receiving a new boundary is confronting. Give it time.

Is there anyone in your life at present that you need to have a boundaries conversation with? If so, describe what you need and why:

....

....

....

....

....

....

....

....

....

....

What are some examples of boundaries you have for yourself?

....

....

....

....

....

....

....

....

....

....

What are some examples of boundaries you have with your family?

What are some examples of boundaries you have for your relationships with new romantic interests, dates, or your partner?

CHOOSE YOUR BOUNDARY RITUAL

Honor Your Boundaries

Write down a list of the words that represent your boundary journey and place them on your altar. When you feel challenged, you can light a candle for yourself and read those words as a reminder.

Protect Your Energy

Visualize a golden bubble of light surrounding you and keeping your energy safe. Draw on this practice in situations where you may struggle to differentiate between your emotional experience and others'.

Cleanse Away the Fears

Have an Epsom salt or sea salt bath. As you soak in the salt, give your fears and worries to the water and allow the salt to ground you in your truth.

Ground Yourself

Anchor yourself by walking barefoot in nature and feeling the connection to the earth beneath you. Remind yourself that it's safe to speak your truth and set boundaries.

Give thanks to all of your past and
present selves who have carried you to
this moment in time.

13

COMING HOME
TO YOURSELF

IN THIS FINAL CHAPTER OF THE JOURNAL, YOU ARE going to bring together all that you have come to know about yourself and deepen in your commitment to your own heart and mind. You have courageously explored your history, your wounds, your growth edges, and the things that make up your unique human experience on this earth. Remember that every version of you from the past is to thank for carrying you to this very moment. We all continue to learn and grow as we move through life. So long as you remain open, all of your experiences can bring you deeper into self-awareness and inner trust.

At your core, you are innocent, loveable, and whole. As you complete the following rituals, may you feel a sense of love, warmth, and self-acceptance emanate from your entire being.

LOVING YOUR PAST AND PRESENT SELF MEDITATION

Find a place to lie down that feels safe and cozy. Bring either a blanket or a comfortable sweater so you are warm and relaxed throughout this practice. Begin by closing your eyes and tuning in to your breath and body.

Visualize yourself *stepping into a beautiful forest. The light is peeking through the trees, and you feel the softness of brilliant emerald moss beneath your feet.*

You walk along a winding path *for some time, surrounded by ancient trees with spiraling roots. As you reach the edge of the forest, imagine yourself as a newborn, wrapped in soft linens in a beautiful nest of leaves and flowers.*

Hold this image in your mind *with tenderness. Beam love toward this new human, who has so much to learn and so many new experiences, lessons, and challenges ahead. Hold yourself with reverence.*

Slowly begin to recall *your first experiences as a small child and different stages of your life, both happy and sad. Allow whatever memories that want to show themselves to come through.*

Witness these memories, *whether they are adventures, losses, heartbreaks, mistakes, or lessons, with the wisdom of a loving and nurturing parent. Hold a space of compassion for the person who was growing, learning, and finding their way. Continue to journey through time with your memories until you find yourself at the present.*

Give thanks to your heart *for beating every single day and bringing you to this very moment. Give thanks to your breath for giving you life. Offer gratitude to all your past selves that had the courage to move through challenges and be here now.*

When you are ready, return to the moment as your present adult self. Acknowledge yourself for all the work you are doing to heal.

HONORING YOUR PAST SELVES

Write a letter to your past selves from a place of compassion and understanding. In this letter speak to yourself with the loving-kindness and warmth you would have wanted from a wise and caring parent.

Dear past _____,

....

....

....

....

....

....

....

....

....

....

....

....

....

....

....

....

....

....

SERAPHINA'S SELF-COMPASSION BATH RITUAL

This beautiful ritual was shared with me by a dear friend and homeopath, Seraphina Capranos. It is a rich blend of soothing and grounding herbs to bring you peace and replenish your soul.

½ cup rose petals

½ cup milky oats

½ cup lavender flowers

To Prepare: Place all the herbs in a pot and cover with 2 inches of water. Simmer for 20 minutes. Then strain and add the hot liquid to a bath. Alternatively, put the herbs in a muslin bag or a nylon sock and tie the herbal bundle to the nozzle of the tub so the running water can flow through them. Once the tub is filled halfway, toss the bundle into the bath like a giant tea bag.

Release and Renew: As you soak in your herbal bath, fill your mind with new belief systems that are compassionate and self-affirming. Allow the aroma of rose petals, milky oats, and lavender flowers to fill you with self-forgiveness. After your bath, consciously pull the plug and allow the bath water to remove all negative, unwanted feelings and beliefs. See them go down the drain, back to the earth, to be composted.

Note: If you are short on time, making an herbal foot or hand bath is also wonderful. Simply adjust the amount of water and herbs to the container size.

WRITING YOUR SACRED SOUL VOWS

*I vow to listen to my body and
trust my instincts.
I vow to make time for personal
healing and growth.
I vow to honor my own boundaries.
I vow to treat my body with love
and kindness.
I vow to speak lovingly to myself.
I vow to care for my inner child.*

Write a letter to your present self. These are your sacred soul vows. What are your commitments to yourself? How will you listen to your body more? How will you care for your own well-being? How will you show up in devotion for the relationship you have with yourself? Write these vows as if you were writing them to a dear lover.

When you are done, you may wish to turn your vows into a piece of art by printing or painting your words and framing them. It can be any form of art or expression you wish. Let this process be unique to you! Then place it somewhere in your home where you will see it every day or on your altar with a flower and a candle. Any time you feel called to sit in presence with yourself, light the candle while you journal or dance or listen to music, and remember these sacred promises you have made to yourself.

Dear _____,

A CLOSING PRAYER

Dear Reader,

To dive deep within is a courageous act, and I bow to you for all the time, energy, and love you have poured into your own inner discovery. Remember that you can come back to the processes in this journal over and over. There is always another layer you can reach. My prayer for you is that you find yourself in a place of true self-acceptance and that you embody your most authentic expression and trust in the divine plan that is your unique life path. If you feel called to continue this work, you may go deeper into each of these topics in my book, *Becoming the One*, or join my online community for daily guidance and inspiration.

May all that you have learned about yourself along this journey serve you in having the most fulfilling relationships and experiencing the greatest joy this life has to offer.

Sheleana Aiyana

ACKNOWLEDGMENTS

THANK YOU TO MY READERS: YOU INSPIRE ME WITH YOUR courage and devotion to knowing yourself. To my wonderful husband, Ben, for all the support you show me when I'm in my writing caves and beyond. Deep gratitude to Eva, my editor: Your genius and eye for detail are so greatly appreciated. To my friend Seraphina, for contributing a beautiful healing recipe to this journal for us all to enjoy. And a special thank-you to all my past teachers who have paved the way before me.

RESOURCES AND RECOMMENDED READING

YOU WILL FIND MORE FREE RESOURCES ON MY WEBSITE
SheleanaAiyana.com and on my social media channels, Instagram, and
YouTube:

>Instagram: @SheleanaAiyana @RisingWoman
>Facebook: @RisingWomanOfficial
>YouTube: @RisingWoman

**Sheleana's husband, Ben, for men's work, addiction counseling,
and conscious relationship:**

>Website: EvolvingMan.com
>Instagram: @EvolvingMan
>YouTube: EvolvingMan

Becoming the One book: RisingWoman.com/BTOBOOK

Herbal and Healing Resources:

>Seraphina Capranos: seraphinacapranos.com
>Canada: Harmonic Arts: harmonicarts.ca
>United States: Mountain Rose Herbs: mountainroseherbs.com

ABOUT THE AUTHOR

SHELEANA AIYANA IS THE INTERNATIONAL BESTSELLING author of *Becoming the One* and the founder of Rising Woman, a growing community of more than three million readers. Her training and immersion in couples facilitation, inherited family trauma, family systems, conscious relationship, somatic healing, and plant medicines inform her holistic approach to seeing relationship as a spiritual path. She lives with her husband, Ben, their daughter, and their dog Bodhi on xʷənen'əč, the unceded land of the Coast Salish peoples, now known as Salt Spring Island, BC.